DIRTY GIRLS
LITTLE BOOK OF JOKES

THIS IS A CARLTON BOOK

Copyright © Carlton Books Limited 2006

This edition published by Carlton Books Limited 2006
20 Mortimer Street
London W1T 3JW

This book is sold subject to the condition that it shall not,
by way of trade or otherwise, be lent, resold, hired out or
otherwise circulated without the publisher's prior written
consent in any form of cover or binding other than that in
which it is published and without a similar condition including
this condition being imposed upon the subsequent purchaser.
All rights reserved.

A CIP catalogue record for this book
is available from the British Library.

ISBN 13: 9-781-84442-182-4
ISBN 10: 1-84442-182-1

Material in this book previously appeared in
The Dirty Girls Joke Book
The Dirty Girls Joke Book 2

Printed in Singapore

DIRTY GIRLS
LITTLE BOOK OF JOKES

CARLTON
BOOKS

INTRODUCTION

Crammed with hilarious gags and one-liners, this handy pocket-sized book is a portable bundle of laughs, with jokes that all fun-loving females can relate to. More than 100 rude and risqué gags and one-liners are included, which are guaranteed to have you giggling, sniggering and splitting your sides in delightful agony. Just don't read it when you've got a face pack on!

LOW EXPECTATIONS

Why do blondes have more fun?

They're more easily impressed.

TOP TIP

What's the definition of a man with a long tongue?

When he sticks it out for the doctor, the nurse goes 'Aaaah!'

FRICTION BURNS

When did Pinocchio realize he was made of wood?

When his hand caught fire.

SORE POINT

Why did the pervert cross the road?

He couldn't get his dick out of the chicken.

PREMATURE ENDING

What's the difference between a curtain and an erection?

A curtain doesn't come down until the performance is finished.

TOOLED UP

How do you know when you're in bed with a blacksmith?

He hammers away for hours and then he makes a bolt for the door.

WELL-ENDOWED INSECT

When John Wayne Bobbit's wife cut off his penis, she drove away with it and threw it out of the car window. Before it landed in the field, it hit the windscreen of another car and bounced off. In the car, a little girl was being driven home by her mother. 'Wow!' said the girl. 'What was THAT?' 'Nothing, honey,' replied her embarrassed mother, 'just a fly.'

'Well,' says the girl, 'for a little fly, it had a huge willy.'

CATCH AN EYEFUL!

What's the difference between a pickpocket and a voyeur?

A pickpocket snatches your watch and a voyeur watches your snatch.

WOULD LIKE TO MEET...

A woman walks into a chemist and asks if they sell extra-large condoms.
'Yes, we do – how many do you want?'
'I don't want to buy any – but if anybody else does, can you give them my phone number?'

FESTIVE ROLE-PLAY

What does a transvestite do at Christmas?

Eat, drink and be Mary.

KEEP IT UP

How do you know when a truckload of Viagra has fallen in the river Thames?

Tower Bridge stays open for hours.

LIFT AND SEPARATE?

A man goes away on a business trip and, as it's a very swanky hotel, his wife comes to join him for the weekend. They have a nice dinner in the restaurant, a drink in the bar, and then they can't wait to go up to their room. In fact, they can't even wait that long – as soon as they get into the lift they're all over each other. The man is pulling her panties down and in less than a minute they're at it.

Unfortunately, the doors open at the next floor and the chambermaid gets in. 'Well, really!' says the chambermaid. 'I'm sorry,' says the woman, 'we just had a couple of drinks and got a bit carried away. I don't normally behave this way.' 'I'm sure you don't,' says the chambermaid, 'but this is the fourth time this week I've caught him at it.'

SWEET SENSATION

What's the difference between a penis and chocolate?

Chocolate's still satisfying after it's gone soft in your hand.

WRONG TURN

Why does only one sperm out of millions get to the egg?

Because they refuse to stop and ask for directions.

GET THE JOB DONE

What's the difference between a man and a lawnmower?

You don't have to suck a lawnmower's exhaust pipe to get it to cut the grass.

SQUEAKY CLEAN

Why doesn't Popeye's favourite tool go rusty?

He puts it in Olive Oil.

A JOB WELL DONE

How do you know when you've given a good blow job?

He has to pull the bed sheets out of his arse.

EVERY LITTLE COUNTS

Why is a man like a dining table?

They both have an extra bit that extends for entertaining.

NICE LITTLE NEST EGG

A woman on her deathbed tells her husband to look in the big trunk under the bed. He opens it and finds three eggs and a thousand pounds in cash. 'Every time I faked an orgasm with you, I took an egg and I put it in the trunk,' says the woman.

'Not bad,' thinks the man, 'three fakes in all these years of marriage.' So he asks the woman, 'But what about the thousand pounds?' 'Every time I got up to a dozen eggs, I sold them.'

THREE LITTLE WORDS (I)

What three words do men hate to hear during sex?

Is it in?

THREE LITTLE WORDS (II)

What three words do women hate to hear during sex?

Honey, I'm home!

FILM FLOP

Why couldn't they get funding for a porn film about flagellation, bestiality and necrophilia?

Everyone said they were flogging a dead horse.

OVER HERE!

John says to his girlfriend, 'Why don't you shout my name out when you come?' she answers, 'Yeah – like you're ever there when I come!'

THE PERFECT PARTNER

What's the difference between a man and a computer?

1. A computer can do more than one job at once.
2. A computer will remember what you told it yesterday.

3. A computer is more impressive the smaller it is.
4. If your computer doesn't have enough hard drive, you can upgrade it.

5. You can still get your work done after you turn a computer on.
6. With a computer, faster is always better.
7. A computer knows the difference between your inbox and your outbox.

8. A computer is more likely to go down on you.
9. A computer can communicate with other computers using words as well as sounds and pictures.
10. A computer can remember important dates like birthdays.

WHO'S THERE?

What does an atheist miss during orgasm?

Somebody to shout at.

GAME ON

Why is sex like playing bridge?

If you don't have a good partner you'd better have a good hand.

MR DIY

A girl takes a guy home. When he takes his pants off, he's got the biggest cock she's ever seen – it reaches down past his knees. 'You want a blow job?' she says, but he replies, 'I'd rather fuck, I can do blow jobs myself.'

EEK!

How does a man make a woman scream in bed?

By wiping his dick on the curtains.

RIDE ON

What's the best thing about sex with a despatch rider?

He's dressed completely in leather and he's really, really dirty.

And the worst thing?

He's always slipping into narrow spaces where you're not meant to go.

NEW AND IMPROVED

What's the difference between a man and a condom?

Condoms aren't thick and insensitive these days.

IDIOT-PROOF

Why do men like blonde girl jokes?

Because they can understand them.

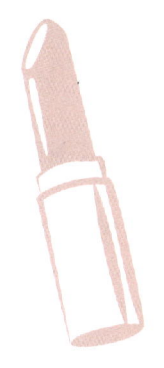

SPREAD THE WORD

How do you know who gives the best cunnilingus?

Word of mouth.

OUCH!

What's the definition of a man with a small penis?

If he walks into a door with an erection he bangs his nose.

SHRINK-WRAPPED

A man walks into the bedroom naked but entirely wrapped in clingfilm and says to his wife, 'Tell me the truth, do you think I'm a pervert?'

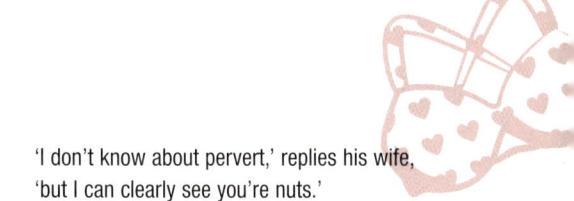

'I don't know about pervert,' replies his wife, 'but I can clearly see you're nuts.'

DRESSING UP

What do you do to make five pounds of fat look sexy?

Put them in a push-up bra.

PLUG AND PLAY

What's the difference between anal sex and a microwave?

A microwave can't turn your meat brown.

SIZE...

According to women, pricks come in three sizes:

Small, medium and ohmigod.

...ISN'T EVERYTHING

According to men, there are still three sizes:

Large, average and size-doesn't-matter

CHECK MATE

A woman goes into a sex shop and asks to see the dildos. The assistant shows her a black one, but she says it's too small. He shows her a pink one, but that's still too small. Then he shows her a chrome one, but she says none of them will do.

Finally, she points to the big tartan one on the top shelf, and says she'll have that one. A few minutes later the manager gets back from lunch and asks how it's going. 'Great – I sold one black dildo, two pink dildos, three chrome dildos – and your Thermos flask.'

SCREEN TEST

What's the difference between cinema snacks and pictures of naked policemen?

One's popcorn and the other's cop porn!

STIFF PENALTY

Why is car insurance cheaper for women?

Because women don't get blow jobs while they're driving.

A SHAGGY DOG STORY

Three women are in the vet's waiting room with their dogs. 'What a lovely labrador,' says one, 'What are you bringing him in for?' 'He is lovely,' says the owner, 'but he's a terrible chewer. He's chewed the furniture and my husband's shoes, but the final straw was when he chewed up my husband's golfclubs and left nothing but a pile of sawdust. So my husband said, either the dog goes, or he goes.' 'So you're having him put to sleep?' 'I'm afraid so,' says the owner.

The second dog is a collie. 'What a lovely collie, what are you bringing him in for?' 'He is lovely but he's a terrible chaser. He chases cars, he chases bicycles, he even chases the postman. The final straw came when he chased my husband's mother down the drive and out of the gate. So my husband said, either the dog goes, or he goes.' 'So you're having him put to sleep?' 'Yes, I'm afraid so.'

So they turn to the third dog. 'What a lovely Great Dane.' 'He is lovely, but he's a terrible shagger. He'll shag anything – the sofa, the neighbour's dog, the vicar's leg. The final straw was when I was getting out of the shower. I bent over to pick up the soap and in no time he was on top of me, shagging away. It took my husband ten minutes to pull him off, and that was it – my husband said, either that dog goes, or I go.'

'So you're having him put to sleep?' 'Oh no, I've just brought him in to have his claws trimmed.'

SICK JOKE

What is warm and soft when a man comes in drunk at night and hard and stiff when he wakes up in the morning?

The pile of puke at the bottom of the stairs.

BITE ME

What's the difference between a masochist and a mosquito?

If you hit a mosquito, it'll stop eating you.

BABY TALK

Why do men call blondes 'dolls'?

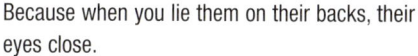

Because when you lie them on their backs, their eyes close.

HOSIERY

A man goes into a party shop and says, 'I'd like to hire a costume, I'm going to a fancy dress party as Adam.' So the assistant gets out a fig leaf: 'There you are sir, that's £5.' 'No, that's not big enough,' he says, so she gets out a bigger one. 'That one's £10.'

'Still not big enough,' he says, so she gets out an even bigger one. 'This one's £15,' she says. 'No, I won't fit into that,' he says, so she gets out a hat that says 'Esso'. 'There,' she says, 'wear this, sling it over your shoulder and go as a petrol pump.'

MEATY QUERY

What's the difference between medium and rare?

Five inches is medium, ten inches is rare.

READ ON

What's the difference between a blonde and a road sign?

Road signs sometimes say 'Stop'.

TURN ME ON

What's white, eight inches long, takes two batteries, gives complete satisfaction in three minutes and once you've tried it you'll never go back to the manual method?

An electric toothbrush.

WHERE THERE'S A WHEEL…

A Hell's Angel drops his motorbike off to be mended, and is walking home. On the way he remembers that he's meant to be picking up some things at the hardware shop for the Hell's Angel Clubhouse. 'Ah, yes,' says the shopkeeper. 'Here you are,' and he gets out a bucket, an anvil, a goat, an axe and a black cockerel.

'How am I meant to carry this lot without my bike?' says the Hell's Angel. 'Well,' says the shopkeeper, 'you could put the cockerel under one arm, the anvil under the other arm, put the axe in the bucket and hold it in one hand, then lead the goat with the other hand.' So the Hell's Angel does as the shopkeeper suggests and starts walking back to the Clubhouse.

A few yards down the road, he's stopped by a little old lady. 'Excuse me, young man,' she says, 'Can you tell me the way to the chapel?' 'It's right next to our clubhouse,' says the Hell's Angel. 'Come with me and I'll show you the way. It's just down this alley.' The old lady looks at him very suspiciously. 'Young man,' she says, 'you are a tall, hairy, muscular man and I am a helpless old woman. How do I know you won't get me half way down that alley, push me roughly against the wall, pull down my panties and take me roughly till your wicked desires are sated?'

'Madam,' he replies, 'I have a bucket in one hand with an axe in it, a goat on a string in the other hand, an anvil under one arm and a cockerel under the other arm, how could I possibly push you roughly against any wall?' So the old lady says, 'Put the cockerel down, put the bucket over the cockerel and the anvil on top of the bucket, lay the axe on the ground and I'll hold on to the goat.'

DOUBLE STANDARDS

When a man talks dirty to a woman it's sexual harassment.

When a woman talks dirty to a man it's £1.60 a minute.

CHEW ON THAT

A woman walks into the dentist's, takes off her knickers and sits in the chair with a leg over each arm. 'Madam, I think there's some mistake,' says the dentist, 'the gynaecologist's surgery is on the next floor.' 'No mistake,' replies the woman. 'Yesterday you put in my husband's new dentures. Today I want you to take them out.'

BEAUTY AND THE BEAST

What do you call a beautiful woman on the arm of an ugly man?

A tattoo.

LIT UP

What's the difference between a blonde girl and a light bulb?

The light bulb is brighter, but the blonde is easier to turn on.

THE MORNING AFTER...

Why is a hangover better than a man?

A hangover is usually gone by lunchtime.

ARMLESS FUN

Two brothers are having a medical, and the doctor comments on the unusual length of their penises. 'Yes, sir, we got them from our mother.' 'Your mother? Surely you inherited them from your father?' 'No, sir. You see our mother only has one arm.'

'One arm? What's that got to do with the length of your penises?'
'Well, she had to lift us out of the bath somehow.'

NEGATIVE THINKING

What's the difference between a man and a battery?

A battery has a positive side.

THAT SINKING FEELING

What's the difference between a blonde girl and the Titanic?

They know how many men went down on the Titanic.

THE MUTT'S NUTS

Two men see a dog licking his own balls. 'I wish I could do that,' says the first man.

'You can,' says the second man, 'if you give him a biscuit first.'

PERIOD DRAMA

Why don't the sanitary towels talk to the tampons?

Because they're stuck up cunts.

BRIDE AND GLOOM

What's a shotgun wedding?

It's a wife-or-death situation.

THE PAINFUL TRUTH

Blonde girl goes to the doctor and says, 'I hurt all over.' She presses her finger into her knee, 'That hurts.' Then she presses her finger into her stomach, 'That hurts,' and then she presses her finger into her forehead, 'Even that hurts. What is it, doctor?'

The doctor replies, 'You have a broken finger.'

DIRTY JOKE

Why are men like cowpats?

The older they get, the easier they are to pick up.

THANKS FOR NOTHING

Why do women get PMT and cellulite?

God made Man first, and he just couldn't help making a few helpful suggestions.

A GOOD RIDE

Why is a bicycle better than a man?

1. You can ride your bicycle for as long as you like, and it won't get there before you do.
2. A bicycle never complains at having to wear rubber tyres.

3. You don't have to shave your legs before you go out on your bicycle.

4. Your parents won't go on about how much they liked your old bicycle.

5. Nothing goes soft on a bicycle that a bicycle pump won't fix.

IT'S ALL IN THE WRIST

A man goes into a chemist and asks for something that will keep him hard all night, as he has a hot date with twin sisters, so the chemist gives him a tube of stay-hard cream. Next day, he's back in the chemist, walking a bit strangely, and asking for a tube of muscle rub. 'You don't want to put muscle rub on your penis,' says the chemist.

'It's not for my penis,' says the man. 'The twin sisters never showed up so this is for my wrist.'

SEX SOCKS

Why do blondes wear knickers?

To keep their ankles warm.

TASTE TEST

What's the difference between pussy and apple pie?

Any man will eat his mother's apple pie.

QUICK AND EASY

Why is a one-night stand like a newsflash?

It's unexpected, brief and probably a disaster.

SNAIL'S PACE

What do snails shout during sex?

'Slower! Slower!'

TOUCHING UP

A newly-wed couple are getting undressed for the first time, and the husband says, 'Darling, your body is so beautiful – let me get my camera and take a picture.' 'Why?' asks his wife. 'So that I can keep it with me always and remember how beautiful you are,' he says.

Then he takes his clothes off and she says, 'Darling, I must also take a photograph of you.' 'Why?' asks her husband. 'So I can get it enlarged,' she replies.

WHO DARES WINS

A man walks into a bar and sees a sign – 'Win Free Drinks for Life' – so he asks the barman how.

'Well,' says the barman, 'You have to pass three challenges. First, you have to drink a bottle of tequila. Next, the landlord's pit bull terrier out in the back yard has toothache – you have to go out and pull that tooth. Finally, the landlord's wife is upstairs and she's never had an orgasm – if you can do the business for her, you get free drinks for life.'

So, the guy thinks he'll give it a try. He takes the bottle of tequila and downs it in one go. Then he staggers out into the back yard. There's terrible growling and snarling, and eventually the guy staggers back in, clawed and scratched all over but grinning from ear to ear.

'Right,' he says, 'that's the first two, now where's that lady with the toothache?'

FELINE FRIENDLY

What's the difference between an unlucky mouse and a lucky cock?

Nothing – they both end up inside a satisfied pussy.

THE UNFAIRER SEX

Why do men like big breasts and tight pussies?

Because they've got big mouths and small pricks.

BABY BOOB

A blonde is walking down the street with her blouse unbuttoned and her right breast hanging out. A policeman stops her and says, 'Madam – are you aware I could arrest you for indecent exposure. You can't walk along the street with your breast hanging out.'

The blonde looks down and says, 'Oh goodness – I left the baby on the bus again!'

HEADS OR TAILS

What's the difference between a man and a ten-pence coin?

Every time you toss the coin, you have a 50/50 chance of getting head.

REAR VIEW

What's the difference between a 69 and driving in fog?

When you're driving in fog, you can't see the arsehole in front of you.

WALKING TALL

One day Bill noticed that his penis had started growing. He was delighted as it rapidly reached six inches, eight inches, then ten inches – and so was his wife. By the time it reached 20 inches, however, Bill was finding it difficult to walk, so they went to see a doctor.

The doctor examined Bill and said that he could carry out corrective surgery. Bill's wife looked worried at this. 'But, Doctor,' she says, 'how long will Bill be in a wheelchair?' 'Dear lady,' says the doctor, 'why should he be in a wheelchair?' 'Well, Doctor,' she replies, 'you are going to lengthen his legs, aren't you?'

WHAT A BANKER!

What's the best thing about sex with a bank clerk?

The bigger the deposit and the longer you leave it in, the more interest you get.

And the worst thing?

He's not so keen on withdrawals.

SIZE MATTERS

Why does an elephant have four feet?

Six inches would look silly on an elephant.

MAN OF FEW WORDS

A couple meet in a bar and end up back at his place. 'You don't talk much,' she says as he's undressing. 'No,' he says, 'I do my talking with this.' 'Sorry,' she says, 'I don't do small talk.'

HEAVEN AND HELL

In Heaven, the lovers are French, the comedians are English and the engineers are German.

In Hell, the comedians are German, the engineers are French and the lovers are English.

THE WILD WEST

Tonto and the Lone Ranger are riding through the desert, when Tonto pulls up his horse and dismounts. He kneels down and presses his ear to the ground, while the Lone Ranger waits in silence.

Finally Tonto raises his head, nods wisely and speaks. 'Buffalo come.' 'Amazing,' says the Lone Ranger. 'Your Indian lore never fails to impress me. Tell me, Tonto, how can you tell?' Tonto speaks again, 'Ear sticky.'

ENERGY DRAIN

Why did the sadist steal the batteries for the vibrator?

Because he liked to take charge.

STRANGE FRUIT

What do you get if you cross a pervert and a hamster?

Letters from animal rights campaigners.

STAND UP GUY…

Who's the most popular man on the nudist beach?

The one who can carry two cups of coffee and six doughnuts.

... AND GAL

Who's the most popular girl on the nudist beach?

The one who can eat the sixth doughnut.

BUMPY RIDE

How do you get some groovy lovin'?

Use a corduroy condom.

HAIRLINE

What's the difference between a clever blonde and a dumb blonde?

The clever blondes have dark roots showing.

SEX MACHINE

What's the difference between a man and a motorbike?

1. You can tell how big the exhaust pipe is before you start riding it.
2. You can swap motorbikes with your friend to see which is the better ride.

3. It's the motorbike that suffers if you don't use enough lubrication.

4. A motorbike stays between your legs till you've had enough fun.

5. You only chain a motorbike up when you've finished riding it.

CLEVER DICK

A woman calls a male escort agency and asks for the most mind-blowing sex she's ever had. They say they'll send over their best stud, Ramon. A while later, the doorbell rings but when she answers the door, she sees a man with no arms and no legs down on the floor.

'I am Ramon,' says the man. 'You?' says the woman. 'How can you give me the most mind-blowing sex I've ever had? You've got no arms and no legs.' 'Listen, lady,' says Ramon, 'I rang the doorbell, didn't I?'

VINTAGE

What's the difference between men and fine wine?

You don't have to roll a man around in your mouth to get the most enjoyment out of him.

SADDLE UP

Why do cowgirls have bow legs?

Because cowboys never take their hats off, even when they're eating.

THIS IS A STICK-UP!

What's the definition of stealing Viagra?

A hold-up by hardened criminals.

SECONDS AWAY

What does a blonde girl do for foreplay?

Warm her ankles.

ANY VOLUNTEERS?

A guy walks into a bar with a crocodile. He sits on a bar stool, gets out a big stick and hits the crocodile once around the head. The crocodile opens its mouth wide, the man unzips his fly, gets his cock out and puts it in the crocodile's mouth.

The man then hits the crocodile again with the stick and it gently closes its mouth, as the whole bar holds its breath. Finally, the man gives the crocodile another sharp tap with the stick. It opens its mouth again and he takes his cock out and puts it back in his pants.

'Right,' he says. 'If anyone else wants to try that, I'll give them a hundred pounds.' Silence. Everyone stares at the crocodile. 'Come on,' says the man, 'a hundred pounds for anyone who'll do it.'

Then a blonde girl pipes up from the back, 'I'll give it a try, but please don't hit me so hard with that stick.'

LADIES ...

Most popular female fantasy?

Having sex with your boyfriend's best friend, a film star, or a stranger on a train.

... AND GENTLEMEN

Most popular male fantasy?

Having sex with a woman who isn't fantasizing about somebody else.

PAINFUL EXPLANATION

Why do sadists take so long to get to the point?

Because they're always beating around the bush.

ONE OFF THE WRIST

What's the difference between an egg and a wank?

You can beat an egg.

MORNING GLORY

What does a blonde do with her arsehole in the morning?

Give him his packed lunch and send him to work.

THE REAL THING

How do you know when you're at a sadist's wedding?

They use real pain for the toasts instead of champagne.

COCK AND BULL

What's the difference between a cockpit and a box office?

A box office is a place that tries to ensure everyone has a satisfying evening's entertainment. A cockpit is really only concerned with getting up and down.

FRENCH CONNECTION

A woman passes a pet shop and sees a sign, 'Clitoris-licking Frog', so she goes in and says, 'I've come about the clitoris-licking frog,' and the assistant answers, 'Oui, Madame?'

BEST OF THREE

What's the difference between embarrassment, worry and panic?

Embarrassment is the first time a man can't get it up a second time.
Worry is the first time he can't get it up for the first time.
Panic is the second time he can't get it up for the first time.

CREATURES OF HABIT

Two nuns are sitting on a bench when a streaker runs past. One has a stroke, but the other one can't reach.

FATAL ATTRACTION

Why is it dangerous to take Viagra and iron tablets?

Every time he gets an erection he ends up pointing North.

SICK AS A PARROT

A woman goes to buy a parrot, and the shopkeeper says, 'We've got one for £100, one for £200 and one for £15.' 'Why is that one so cheap?' asks the woman. 'Well, it used to live in a brothel, so it's a bit foulmouthed.' The woman says she doesn't mind, so she pays her £15 and takes the parrot home.

As soon as she takes the cover off the cage, the parrot says, 'Fuck me, a new brothel!' Then he looks at the woman and says, 'Fuck me, a new Madam!' 'I am not a Madam, and this is not a brothel,' says the woman, but she thinks it's quite funny.

Later on, her two teenage daughters come in. 'Fuck me,' says the parrot, 'new prostitutes!' 'We are not prostitutes,' say the daughters, but they think it's quite funny too. 'Wait till Dad comes in and hears this parrot, he'll go spare.'

So they put the parrot in the hall, the door opens and Dad comes in. Dad looks at the parrot, and the parrot looks at him, then the parrot says, 'Fuck me, Dave, haven't seen you for weeks.'

HIDDEN MEANING (I)

When men say, 'Do you have any fantasies?' they mean,

'Can we try anal sex/you dressing up as Batgirl/ a threesome with your sister?'

HIDDEN MEANING (II)

When women say, 'Do you have any fantasies?' they mean:

'I'm so bored that, frankly, I'll try anything.'

SEX SIRENS

Why is a woman like a police car?

They both make a lot of noise to let you know they're coming.